Shannon—
You are amazing
and such a treasure
to me and the Kingdom
of God! Love you so much!
♡ Noma

One fine morning

A 30 DAY DEVOTIONAL

NOMA HEDMAN

Dedicated to my amazing family...
Eric, my person, who loves me without condition and pushes me to pursue the call of God on my life and has allowed me the freedom to do ALL that God says I can. Thank you for believing in me and in all of my dreams.
Austin, Maddy, and Naomi... my greatest gifts and treasures from the Father. I would choose each one of you. You are my favorite people and I am the most blessed woman to be yor mom.

Thank you's:
Pastors Scott and LeAnn Smith my forever mentors and friends. Thank you for giving me my first ministry opportunity and for always declaring the Word of God over my life. I am so gratefulul for your leadership and your friendship. I am so blessed to count you as not only friends but family. Love you guys!

Pastors Dan and Terry Hammer my pastors, mentors, and spiritual parents. Thank you for your unrelenting love for Jesus and His people. You make church and life fun! Thank you for your encouragement, prayers, and belief in me.

Pastors John & Grace Hammer...thank you for representing Jesus so well and for your constant support and encouragement. You guys are awesome!

Pastors Andre and Ambra Benjamin...thank you for bringing the "Eye of the Tiger" to everything you do! I feel so blessed to be able to glean from you both. Thank you for championing me in my purpose.

My sister friend Tara...we were destined to do life together. Thank you for your constant kick in the pants and for pushing me to accomplish what is in my heart. Thank you for our writing challenge and your miraculous publishing skills around the campfire! Love you Sissy!

Dear Friend,

Coffee, Jesus, and the Word. Three of my favorite things all put together...One Fine Morning. This devotional was birthed out of a call to meet Jesus for coffee and taken from my personal devotion times with Him. Some are personal and some are challenging. My prayer is that all will lead you to a deeper place with Him. Will you join me in meeting Him? Grab your Bible, your favorite cup of joe and have one fine morning. Blessings on the journey.

Noma

Day 1
The Journey Begins
Psalm 143:8

"Cause me to hear Your loving-kindness in the morning, For in You do I trust; Cause me to know the way in which I should walk, For I lift up my soul to You."

I never would have thought that I would ever call myself a morning person. I've always been somewhat of a night owl. Late nights in college led to late nights with babies and then late nights with the teenagers. I found myself always running and struggling to have time with Jesus. I would do really well for a while, finding time here and there, but nothing ever stuck. I would do my devotion time while my kids did their homeschooling...not really focused and undivided attention on the Lord. My teenagers went back to traditional high school this past year and so became my perfect opportunity for one on one time with Jesus...that is if I could get it before the toddler woke up. I decided that I would get up, see my kids off, and then I would spend time with Jesus. Well, coffee and Jesus. I began having coffee with Jesus every morning. I love mornings now. I enjoy getting up knowing that I get to spend time with my Jesus. We have coffee together, and He speaks to me. He does show me the way in which I should walk as I lift up my life to Him.

Take a journey with me. For the next 29 days, get up early or whatever time you start your day, grab your coffee, and spend time with Jesus. You will see a difference in your day, attitude, energy, and spirit. You won't regret it. If you don't know my Jesus, I encourage you to discover who He is and how much He deeply loves you. If you do know Him, I pray that you will come to know Him at an even deeper level. I pray you are encouraged and challenged as we take the next 29 days to get into the Word and hear His loving-kindness in the morning.

Take some time and write down what you are seeking the Lord for and what you need and want to hear from Him. Write down Your goals for this journey and refer back to it as we go along.

Prayer Starter

Lord, I long to hear your loving-kindness. I long to know You more. I lift up my soul to You and ask that You would lead me and guide me. Speak to me through this journey and reveal truth to my heart.

journal

journal

Day 2
"Be a Doer"

James 1:22-25

"But be doers of the word, and not hearers only, deceiving yourselves. 23 For if anyone is a hearer of the word and not a doer, he is like a man observing his natural face in a mirror; 24 for he observes himself, goes away, and immediately forgets what kind of man he was. 25 But he who looks into the perfect law of liberty and continues in it, and is not a forgetful hearer but a doer of the work, this one will be blessed in what he does."

The word of God is living and active. It is good for every part of life. What does it mean to be a doer of the word? To be a doer of the word we need to allow the word to work in us and change us. It means to walk it out. The word of God is a mirror for us. It shows us who we are and what we look like. When we don't walk it out and live it, we can easily forget who we are and what we are to look like. How many times a day do we check our reflection? How often do we check to make sure our hair is in place, our makeup is right, that we don't have anything in our teeth, and on and on? We even catch our reflection as we pass windows and do a quick check. So too, we should be checking our spiritual mirror. We should have the word in our hearts and before our eyes so that when things come up in our day we can do a quick check. We can pull out our mirror and be sure our attitudes are in place, our motives are right, and that we don't have anything that would mess up our reflection. We are to be a reflection of Christ.

We are to be a doer of the work and word in us. It's active...it's actively living and walking out the work He is doing in us so that when we catch our reflection, we see Jesus. We cannot allow ourselves to forget who we are and what we are to look like.

I have a question for you. What are you reflecting? When you look at yourself through the looking glass of the word what do you see? Do you recognize your face? Do you remember who you are? Be honest with yourself today and really check your reflection. Are you being a doer of the work in you or have you been a hearer only? Choose today to activate that work and walk it out. Don't forget who you are and what you look like. Spend time in front of the mirror and see the beautiful reflection of Jesus in you.

Daily Declarations:

I declare that I am not a hearer only, but that I am a doer of the work He is doing in me. I declare that I know who I am and I declare that I am the reflection of Christ.

Prayer Starter

Lord, Thank You for Your word. Thank You that it is alive, active, and working in me. Thank You for making me a reflection of Jesus. Help me to not forget who I am or what I look like. In Jesus' name, Amen.

journal

journal

Day 3
"Are You A Slave"

Galatians 4:7

"Therefore you are no longer a slave but a son, and if a son, then an heir of God through Christ."

This verse caught me today and forced me to answer the question, "Are you a slave?" My first response would be No! I am a believer and free in Christ! Then the Holy Spirit showed me the truth in my heart which is yes-I am a slave.

Hard to admit when you work hard to be all that you know God says you are. In my heart I know the truth. I am a slave. I have been a slave the majority of my life. I am enslaved by my weight. I have struggled and been overweight most of my life, it is something I have never been able to conquer. Today I realized that the reality of my weight issue is that it is an issue of slavery. I have allowed myself to become a slave of my own body. I have never called it for what it is, but the truth is, I have lived as a slave.

Today, the Spirit of God gave me the revelation that because I am a daughter of God that I am no longer a slave-this includes to myself. I think so often we base whether we are slave or free on the lifestyle we lead; whether it is sinful or not. We have our lists of dos and don'ts and as long as we are living Godly, we are free. Sometimes we don't realize that the things we down play or write off as just being who we are is really enslaving us.

Often times it is easier to walk in the Spirit and in the fruit of the Spirit towards others than it is to walk this way toward ourselves. The Lord also showed me that I need to demonstrate

16

love, joy, peace, patience, kindness, goodness, faithfulness, gentleness, and self-control to myself just as much as I do with others.

The Word of God brings life to every part of our hearts and lives. It shines the light on the dark places that we do not know are there and when things are brought out of the dark freedom is found. I found freedom today. I am a daughter of the Almighty living God. My body does not own me or control me.

Will you join me in freedom today? You may not be enslaved by weight, but let the Holy Spirit shine the light on every area of your heart and life. You are no longer a slave. Be free... Choose freedom!

Daily Declarations:

I declare that I am no longer a slave to _____, but I am a son/daughter of the Most High. I am a joint heir with Christ and my freedom was bought at a price. I declare that I am free from the lies of the enemy that would say "this is just how I am". No! I renounce my agreement with that and declare freedom over my life!

Prayer Starter

Thank You Lord for Your word. Thank You that Your truth sets me free. Help me to choose freedom every day. In Jesus' name, Amen

journal

journal

Day 4
"The Invitation"

Isaiah 55:1-3

"Ho! Everyone who thirsts, come to the waters; and you who have no money, Come, buy and eat. Yes, come, buy wine and milk without money and without price. Why do you spend money for what is not bread, and your wages for what does not satisfy? Listen carefully to Me, and eat what is good, and let your soul delight itself in abundance. Incline your ear, and come to Me. Hear and your soul shall live; and I will make an everlasting covenant with you- The sure mercies of David."

This is an invitation. An invitation, a call, a beckoning. Come...An invitation for everyone. This invitation is no respecter of persons. Every-one come. Come, all who thirst. All! Even those with nothing to give. How do you buy some-thing with no money and no price? You don't, it's given. God is calling all to come. No matter the deficiency, He's saying come. In spite of the deficiency, come. Abundance is waiting. This is an invitation and call to put off those things that would waste our time and keep us unful-filled and unsatisfied. Only He can truly satis-fy. Only He can fulfill and complete us. This is not only a call to put off those things, but it's a call and invitation to delight in His abun-dance. Abundant life, fulfillment, and provi-sion. He has provided it all and it's all waiting.

He is inviting you to come. Come with your deficiencies. He has more than enough. He has already paid the price. Stop wasting your time and energy on things that aren't in His plan for you. He is calling you to listen carefully, lean in, and hear Him. He has amazing things for you. He has abundant life. A full life. A meaningful life. A called life. An anointed life. We are all called to come. We are all called to abundant life. Despite our deficiencies, which

He already knows; He calls us to come to Him. He promises good things when we do.

What are the deficiencies in your life? What are the things that waste your time and leave you unfulfilled? Are you willing to come and exchange those things for abundant life? Abundant life extends beyond salvation and beyond finances. Abundant life in every part of life. He is extending an invitation...Come. No matter the deficiency...Come. I hope you make a beautiful exchange today. Come...

Daily Declarations

I declare that I walk in abundant life. I declare abundance over every part of my life. I declare that I am exchanging my deficiencies for God's abundance. I declare that I will lack no good thing.

Prayer Starter

Lord, Thank You for inviting me to come to You regardless of the deficiencies in my life. Thank You for abundant life. Help me to cast off the things that waste my time and keep me from pursuing abundant life. I choose to exchange my deficiencies for Your abundance. In Jesus' name, Amen

journal

journal

Day 5
"Press, Forget, Reach"

Philippians 3:12-14

"Not that I have already attained, or am already perfected; but I press on, that I may lay hold of that for which Christ Jesus has also laid hold of me.[13] Brethren, I do not count myself to have apprehended; but one thing I do, forgetting those things which are behind and reaching forward to those things which are ahead, [14] I press toward the goal for the prize of the upward call of God in Christ Jesus."

Press on, forget what's behind, reach forward, press toward. Each phrase is a key element to these verses and they are keys to fulfilling the purpose God has on your life. Press on...Keep on keeping on. Even though the work in you is still being perfected. Keep pressing on. I heard it said once, "Don't wait to be great, to be great". This is so good! We aren't to wait and linger where we are but we are to press on, keep walking, and keep going. Press on and forget what's behind. Leave your past behind you. Learn from it and press on.

Many times the hurts, abuses, sins, accomplishments, victories, and fulfillments of the past keep us from moving into the next thing God has for us. We get stuck in a defining moment of our lives and have a hard time letting go. We hold on and allow the hurts and abuses to define and change our identity. We become victim to our circumstances and to the people who have hurt us. We become locked up in fear and hurt all the while the enemy is using that thing to change our name and he hopes our destiny. This tactic of the enemy has been successful with too many and it angers me.

Many people live stuck; believing that they can not live greater than what has happened to them and the choices they have made. Regret is no way to live. You are not what has happened to you. You are not a victim of life but you are a conqueror of life. Look how far you've come. Now look ahead at all that's ahead. You have a wonderful future waiting for you. It's time to stop looking back, stop holding on to a wrong identity. It is time to start reaching forward. You can't reach forward while you are reaching back. Leave the things behind and reach forward to what is ahead. Press toward the goal.

What are the dreams in your heart? What are the dreams that got stuck? It's time to awaken those dreams and press toward them. We are to reach toward the upward call of God in Christ Jesus. What is it that God has prepared for you to do? Ask Him and He will reveal it to you. Remember you are a child of God. You are accepted. You are loved. You are redeemed. You are free. You are not a slave. You are not what has happened to you. You are victorious! Press on, forget what's behind, reach forward, press toward...Your life and destiny are waiting, and it's good.

Daily Declarations

I declare that I am a child of God. I declare that I have a destiny. I declare that I am not a victim of circumstances or life. I declare that I am victorious. I declare that I am free from the past. I declare that I am moving forward.

Prayer Starter

Lord, thank You for my life. Thank You for all You have brought me through. Today I choose life. I choose to stop reaching back and to start reaching forward. Help me to keep my eyes on You. In Jesus' name, Amen.

journal

journal

Day 6
"Community"

Romans 1:11-12

"For I long to see you, that I may impart to you some spiritual gift, so that you may be established- that is that I may be encouraged together with you by the mutual faith both of you and me."

What is community? Webster gives one definition of community as "a feeling of fellowship with others, as a result of sharing common attitudes, interests, and goals". That is what we are as the body of Christ. We are not meant to walk this out alone. We are not to think ourselves so mature that we have no need of others. Maturity comes in community. It is where it is nurtured and fed. Community is important and necessary for growth and, each one of us has a gift to share and impart. Each one of us needs to be established and encouraged. This only comes through community. Community is where we are built up and held accountable. Accountability is vital to the life and maturity of the believer. This is what Paul is writing about.

We build each other up and strengthen each other's faith when we meet together and share in the Word and in fellowship. Paul knew that not only did he have a gift to bring and impart but that he would benefit from the faith and gifts that the others in the community brought. We all have something to contribute. We all play an important part in the assignment God has on our local body. We each are an important piece to the puzzle. When one piece is not in place the puzzle is not complete. You are needed and valuable to fulfilling the call on your place of community. Whether in few or in many, community is important and necessary. If you don't have a church or a home group that you belong to, find one.

Get planted. Get involved. Your piece is needed. You could very well be the missing piece that will complete the puzzle.

Daily Declarations

I declare that I have a part to play in community. I declare that I will grow and mature in a place of community. I declare that my church, home group, or ministry with be complete with all the pieces doing their part.

Prayer Starter

Thank you Lord for the reminder that I have a part to play and that my part is valuable. Thank You for my church and my leaders. Help me to find the place that my piece fits. Thank You for the gifts You have given me and for the purpose on my life. Help me to fulfill my part in community. In Jesus' name, Amen

journal

journal

Day 7

"He Knows You"

Jeremiah 29:11

"For I know the thoughts I think toward you, says the Lord, thoughts of peace and not of evil, to give you a future and a hope."

The Lord thinks of you. He knows you. He sees you. The One who holds all of time and space, knows you. The One who formed the mountains and gave the oceans their boundaries knows you. He is the King of Kings and the Lord of lords and He knows you. He knows every part of you. He has even numbered the hairs on your head. He loves you and He knows you. It's incredible! He is an intentional God. He does nothing on accident. You were created with purpose and intention. He has a plan for you. He is not only intentional but He is individual. He sees you. You are not just part of the crowd but He sees you right where you are and He knows you. He knows your name, He knows your heart; He knows your past, your present, and your future. Nothing that has happened or will happen is a surprise to Him. You are not forgotten. You are present in His thoughts. He knows the thoughts He has toward you and of you and they are good. He has a plan for you. Trust Him. He holds the universe in place surely He can hold your heart. He is a good God and a trustworthy God. We can trust that He will perform the thoughts He has towards us.

Daily Declarations

I declare that I am known by God. I am on purpose and have a purpose. I declare that I trust the intentions of God's heart towards me. I declare that I am His!

<u>Prayer Starter</u>:

Thank You Lord for being an intentional and individual God. Thank You for knowing me and for loving me. I trust You and I trust Your heart towards me. I trust Your plan. You are good and I love You.

journal

journal

Day 8
"But God"

Ephesians 2:1-7

"And you He made alive, who were dead in trespasses and sins, in which you once walked according to the course of this world, according to the prince of the power of the air, the spirit who now works in the sons of disobedience, among whom also we all once conducted ourselves in the lusts of the flesh, fulfilling the desires of the flesh and of the mind, and were by nature children of wrath, just as the others. But God, who is rich in mercy, because of His great love with which He loved us, even when we were dead in trespasses, made us alive together with Christ (by grace you have been saved), and raised us up together, and made us sit together in the heavenly places in Christ Jesus, that In the ages to come He might show the exceeding riches of His grace in His kindness toward us in Christ Jesus."

This passage is amazing as it speaks of who we once were and then with two words who we once were changed. I love words. I love the power of words. I love the beauty of words. I also love the times when words fail. Usually those are the times when only The Word can bring comfort. I was struck in this passage by two words. "But God". Small but powerful words. These two words shift and change identity, situations, and the direction of life. This passage says, "we walked according to the course of this world, But God..." We were dead in our sin But God, out of His love for us, made us alive! Bam! Two words changed the course of life. "But God!"

There is a "But God" for any situation you face. Things may look really bad...But God..."works all things together for good to those who love Him and are called according to His purpose". That is you and me! It may look like there is no way...But God..."will make a way when there seems to be no way." You may be lacking provision...But God..."shall supply all of your needs according to His riches in glory." You may be in turmoil...But God...will give you the "peace that passes all understanding." You may be sick...But God..."shall arise with healing in His wings." You may be in a situation where you need favor...But God..."holds the heart of the king in His hands and turns it to whomever He desires."

Whatever situation you face today find your "But God", declare it over that thing and see Him do great and mighty things on your behalf!

Daily Declarations

I declare that I am alive in Christ. I declare that I sit in heavenly places with Christ Jesus. I declare that God is able to work all things to my good. I declare that He will supply all of my need. I declare that I am healed and that the peace of God guards my heart and mind. I declare I walk in the favor of the Lord.

Prayer Starter

Lord, thank You for Your word. Thank you for the power of Your word. I trust You in every situation I face today. Help me to find the "But God" to everything that would come against me.

journal

journal

Day 9
"Beautiful Timing"

Ecclesiastes 3:11

"He has made everything beautiful in its time. Also He has put eternity in their hearts, except that no one can find out the work that God does from beginning to end."

Everything has a season and every season has a purpose. Seasons come and seasons go, the key for us is how we walk in the season we are in. What is our attitude and our motivation in each season we face? Many times we can be in a season for a long time and we begin to resent it and lose patience and heart. We forget that all seasons have beauty in them. We forget to look around and enjoy what God is doing in the current season and we forget to look for the signs of the coming one.

One day in the early part of March I was leaving for work. I walked out of my house with my toddler in tow and realized the tree in my front yard was fully in bloom. The only thing is that I had not even noticed that the tree had been budding and preparing for spring. Spring came early for us this year. I had been so caught up in life and coming and going that I did not notice the change happening right before me. The Lord spoke to me and taught me something in that moment. He said, "Stop getting so caught up in the season you are in that you forget to look around at the beauty of what I am doing and start to look for the signs of the new season".

Each season we are in produces life if we let it. The end of each season buds into the blooms of the new one. What are you focusing on in the current season you are in? What is the Lord wanting to bring to life and full bloom? Remember that we only see in part. We may not see the whole picture beginning to end but He will make every part of the journey a beautiful adventure. Even in times when He seems far away the beauty lies in the pursuit of Him. In times of sorrow the beauty is in His comfort and peace. In times of rejoicing the beauty is in His goodness. In times of confusion the beauty is in His wisdom and word. There is beauty in every season. We just have to stop and look for it. Choose today to look for the beauty of the season you are in and choose to look for the signs of change. Don't get so stuck in the place you are at that you don't see the change of season coming.

Daily Declarations

I declare that there is beauty in the season I am in. I declare life to every part of my season. I declare that God is working a good thing in this season and I declare that I am watching and waiting for the beauty of the coming season.

Prayer Starter

Thank You Lord for Your word. Thank You that You want to bring beauty and life to every season I walk through. Help me to see the beauty of what You are doing. Thank You for being with me and guiding me through every season of life.

journal

journal

Day 10
"Masterpiece"

Ephesians 2:10

"For we are His workmanship created in Christ Jesus for good works, which God prepared beforehand that we should walk in them".

An artist has the artistic ability even before anything is painted on the canvas, written on the page, seen through the camera's eye, played on the keys, strummed on the strings, sung or spoken. You too are the express representation of God's ability even though you're still being perfected. Ephesians 2:10 says, "For we are His workmanship created in Christ Jesus for good works, which God prepared beforehand that we should walk in them". The amazing part we play is that we get to choose what we become. We can choose to let Him work His masterpiece in us regardless of how long it takes or we can try to finish the work on our own and not see the fulfillment of what the artist intended.

Sometimes the masterpiece takes a while. Sometimes the film has to be developed a bit longer. It all depends on the vision in the heart of the artist. God has an amazing vision for your life and the masterpiece you are. What will you choose? Will you allow the original artist to work the masterpiece in you? Think over times when you've tried to take control over the process? How did that work out for you? The beautiful thing is that you still get the choice. Take some time and write out what stage of the process you're in. Do you see the masterpiece being formed or is it still in the beginning stages? Whatever stage of the process you're in know that it is His hand sculpting and molding you. You can trust Him and you can trust the process.

Daily Declarations

I choose today to remain in the hand of Him who will complete the masterpiece in me. I choose to remain on the canvas and in the dark room until I become exactly what He envisioned me to be.

Prayer Starter

Dear Lord, I trust You as You work in me. I trust You in the process. Help me to not take my process out of Your hands. I thank You for the good works You have prepared for me. Help me to walk in them the way You have designed me to.

journal

journal

Day 11
"Stand Still"

Exodus 14:13-14

"And Moses said to the people, 'Do not be afraid. Stand still, and see the salvation of the Lord, which He will accomplish for you today. For the Egyptians whom you see today, you shall see again no more forever. The Lord will fight for you, and you shall hold your peace.'"

Whatever you are facing today know that the Lord goes before you. All you have to do is stand still, hold your peace, and see His salvation. He is a faithful Father who keeps His covenant promises to us. He will fight for you, and when you know in your knower that the Almighty God is working on your behalf then you can hold your peace. We are to hold on to peace and not let go. When we let go of peace, it's easy to pick up worry, fear, and doubt. We are to stand still in the peace of knowing who the battle really belongs to. When we do this we will see His salvation come. He will perform that which is needed. Trust and know that He will bring it to pass. Hold on to peace today. He loves you and will keep His promises to you. He is always faithful to perform His word!

Have you been letting go of peace lately? What are the things that cause you to let go? Write down those things and declare victory!

Daily Declarations

I declare that I am a person that holds on to peace. I declare that the battle is the Lord's and I trust that He is fighting for me. I declare that I trust Him. I declare that He is faithful!

Prayer Starter

Thank You Lord for fighting on my behalf. Thank You for the peace I can hold on to in knowing You have it under control. I choose to stand still and see Your salvation.

journal

journal

Day 12

"From King to Slave"

Philippians 2:5-8 (MSG)

"He had equal status with God but didn't think so much of Himself that He had to cling to the advantages of that status no matter what. Not at all. When the time came, He set aside the privileges of deity and took on the status of a slave, became human! Having become human, he stayed human. It was an incredibly humbling process. He didn't claim special privileges. Instead, He lived a selfless, obedient life and then died a selfless, obedient death-and the worst kind of death at that-a crucifixion."

Wow! I love this passage and I love it as it is written in the Message Bible. I am a diehard New King James girl but I love the language and the simplistic way this passage is in the Message. Here we see that Jesus, equal with God and Himself being God, sets aside His kingship, steps off His throne, and humbles Himself to the status of a slave...He, the King of Kings and the Lord of lords, becomes human. He willingly gave up His position, His deity and was born one of us. He didn't flaunt who He was or call down angels from heaven in a display of entitlement. No, He emptied Himself to the point of death. He lived and died the same way. Selfless and obedient. Why? Why would a King give up their throne? Why would He set aside the joy of His Father and take on the sin of the world? Why? So we too could be the joy of His Father. The word says that for the joy set before Him He endured the cross. We were that joy. You and me. He did it all for us. He did it all and paid the ultimate price so that we could be reconciled to the Father. Oh how He loves us! Both Jesus and the Father love us with such a remarkable love that they willingly gave. The Father gave His Son and Jesus gave His life. All for the love of us. Jesus died a horrific death so that no longer could sin separate us from the love of Him and the Father. Eternity changed forever that blessed, horrible, and terrific weekend. The mourning of Friday turned to the dancing of Sunday as Jesus, no longer dead and buried but He arose alive and victorious! He forever holds the keys of sin and death and He reigns forever. He is now back on His throne at the right hand of the Father and He is awaiting us. He is awaiting the day when He will come with a shout and trumpet sound to bring us home to the Father with Him! What a glorious day that will be!

Daily Declarations

Today's declarations are your own. Declare your thankfulness for what Jesus has done and for how much He loves you.

Prayer Starter

Father, Thank You for sending Your son. Jesus, thank You for coming so willingly. Thank You for Your sacrifice. Thank You for loving me so completely.

journal

journal

Day 13
"Who Are You?"

Read Luke 4:1-13

In this passage we find Jesus being led into the wilderness where He is tempted by the devil. Notice the wording in verses three and nine. The devil says to Jesus, "If You are the Son of God..." The temptation started with a question of identity. The identity, the sonship, the truth of who Jesus was, was questioned. The identity and the authority that came with His identity was brought into question when the devil tempted Him with authority. This is what the enemy would do with us. He gets us to question our identity so we don't walk in the authority our identity carries. He keeps us in an identity crisis all the while he is wreaking havoc.

Jesus showed us the way out of temptation and the crisis of identity. Speak the truth! When the enemy would question your identity-you speak the truth of who you are. You are a son, a joint heir with Christ. All authority has been given to you so walk in it. Does the general of an army identify himself as a private? No! Does the President identify himself as the secretary of state? No! Their position and the identity of their position brings them authority. No longer can we surrender our authority by questioning our identity. No longer can we identify ourselves as less than who we are. It is time to speak the truth and give zero tolerance for the enemy!

What is it that the enemy uses to question your identity and authority? Identify those things so you can declare truth when he comes to battle you. For every question of identity there is an answer in the Word. Find those answers and declare them constantly over your life. The enemy has to flee when resisted.

Daily Declarations

I declare that I am child of the Most High God. I am a joint heir with Christ. I declare that I resist the lies of the enemy and he has to flee. I will no longer surrender my authority by believing a lie.

Prayer Starter

Dear Lord, Thank You that my identity is found in You. I thank You that have prepared truth for me. I ask that You would open my eyes to see and my ears to hear the lies and attack of the enemy against my identity. Help me to speak the truth and walk in my true identity and authority.

journal

journal

Day 14
"Children of Light"

Ephesians 5:8-11

"For you were once darkness, but now you are light in the Lord. Walk as children of light (for the fruit of the Spirit is in all goodness, righteousness, and truth), finding out what is acceptable to the Lord. And have no fellowship with the unfruitful works of darkness, but rather expose them."

The Lord is so good to illuminate and shine light on His word to bring fresh revelation. "Walk as children of light". How do we do this? What does it mean to walk as children of light? I believe it goes beyond just not sinning. It goes beyond living according to the law. So, what does it mean? By walking in the fruit of the Spirit, we walk in the light. All of the fruit of the Spirit rest in goodness, righteousness, and truth. Three things to test whether we are walking as children of light. Is it good? Is it righteous? Is it true? How do we know what is acceptable to the Lord? By knowing Him. By daily being transformed by the renewing of our minds. Asking those questions, Is it good, Is it righteous, and Is it true? will lead to finding what is acceptable to Him. Be in His word. Let His word illuminate and expose the areas that are unfruitful. This is something to do daily. We are to daily pick up our cross and follow Him. It's not a burden but it's daily choosing to walk in the light. It is allowing Him to shine the light on our lives and in our hearts and minds. As we find out the things that are acceptable to Him we need to be willing to let go and walk away from the things that are unfruitful in our lives. The Scripture says to have no fellowship with those things. Many times we don't even know we are allowing unfruitful things to buddy up to us. This is why it is so important that we spend time with Him every day. Don't allow the unfruitful things to fellowship with you. As you walk in the light and the fruit of the Spirit exposes the things that are not good, righteous, and true; call them for what they are and "break up" with them! It could be attitudes, sin issues, insecurities, doubt, fear, or pride. Anything that is contrary to what is good, righteous, and true. It's time to shine the light into all the deep reaches of our hearts and minds. Let's choose today to always walk as children of light. Expose those things that would want to creep in and bring unfruitfulness in your life. Remember if it's not good, righteous, or true it does not belong to you!

Daily Declarations

I declare that I am a child of light. I declare that I live and walk in the fruit of the Spirit. I choose to "break up" with those things that would bring unfruitfulness in my life. I declare goodness, righteousness, and truth over my life.

Prayer Starter

Lord, You are so good! Thank You for Your word. Help me to walk in what is good, righteous, and true. Show me the things in my life that are unfruitful. I ask that You shine Your light into the deep places of my heart and reveal anything that is not of You.

journal

journal

Day 15
"Who Do You Trust?"

Proverbs 3:5-6

"Trust in the LORD with all your heart, And lean not on your own understanding; In all your ways acknowledge Him, And He shall direct your paths."

The Lord gave me a picture of the word trust. The letters stood tall and bold. They were cast in gold with a beautiful filigree design. Trust is really a big and beautiful thing. It involves your heart and your mind. Trust is a choice. Webster defines trust as, "assured reliance on the character, ability, strength or truth of someone or something: one in which confidence is placed." In order to fully trust someone with all your heart you have to know them. You have to know their character. You have to be confident in who they are. So in order for us to really trust the Lord we have to know Him. How have you been trusting lately? We have to be so careful that we don't deflect our disappointments with others onto the Lord. We cannot measure the Lord against a failed standard. He sets the standard. He is true, kind, gracious, loving, strong, and able. We have to know Him to trust Him. He never fails. He never lies. He can't lie. It's impossible. The Word says that God is not a man that He should lie. He will not lie to you. He will never break His promises. He will never leave you. We can put all of our confidence in Him. Sometimes we are in a season of trusting. In those seasons it's so important to tune our ears to hear His voice and tune our hearts to hear His heart. When you're not seeing you have to hone your other senses to know where He is leading. Remember He cannot lie. His voice of truth cancels out every doubt, every fear, and every lie. We can trust Him. We can trust that He is who He says He is. We can trust His heart with our hearts. He will lead you as you trust Him.

Trust Him with your whole heart; even when you're not seeing.

A sweet couple in the church I grew up in used to sing a song called "Trust His Heart". Many times in my life when things have happened that would want to shake my confidence and trust in Him, the lyrics of that song would flood my mind. "When you don't understand, when you can't see the plan, when you can't trace His hand, trust His heart." This is what it's about. Having assurance and confidence in the heart and character of God. When we know Him and His heart we can trust Him. How are you trusting Him today? Do you trust Him according to a failed standard? Do you know Him? Take time to know His heart today. Take time to hear His voice. Take time to hear His heart. He loves you and He is trustworthy.

Daily Declarations

I declare that I will trust the Lord. I declare that I will choose to trust Him. I declare that He is trustworthy and that He keeps His promises.

Prayer Starter

Lord, thank You that I can trust You. Lead me today as I put my trust in You. Help me to not measure you against a failed standard. You are good. You are true. Thank You for holding my heart. I trust You Lord. In Jesus' name, Amen.

journal

journal

Day 16

"Perspective"

Colossians 3:23-24

"And whatever you do, do it heartily, as to the Lord and not to men, knowing that from the Lord you will receive the reward of the inheritance; for you serve the Lord Christ."

I love that these verses are found in a group of verses under the heading "The Christian Home". The verses leading up to this nugget are talking to wives, husbands, children, and fathers. I find it interesting that after we are told to submit, love, obey, and not provoke that we are reminded to do everything as to the Lord. I think it's there because God knows the struggle is real. Some days it's a real struggle to pick those socks up...AGAIN; to work overtime...AGAIN; to obey... AGAIN. Sometimes the daily tasks become burdens and we can become resentful. So to keep us from becoming resentful God gives us this nugget. This promise of reward. Nothing we do is in vain when we do it unto the Lord. When we are serving our families we are serving the Lord. Our first calling and ministry is to our families. Sometimes we just have to shift our perspective. Instead of seeing all the stuff that has to be done as a burden, we need to see it as a ministry. Even obedience to parents is a ministry. I know it pleases and blesses my heart when my kids obey. This shift of perspective is a choice to make daily, hourly, and let's be real, sometimes minute by minute.

Every day we have a choice. We choose our perspective, our attitude, and our behavior. We can choose to do all things as unto the Lord. It's hard sometimes, but it is possible. Now, I'm not saying that every day birds will be singing around you as you do the dishes or as you do your work. No, sometimes the sound is a toddler's temper tantrum, a teenager's slammed door, or the loud sound of silence. We don't live in a Disney movie. I don't have little woodland animals helping me clean house. Although that would be pretty cool. There are days when it's really hard to keep the right attitude when you've cleaned the living room for the fourth time. I know. It's a daily struggle. What I'm saying is that we can choose how we deal with the struggle. We can stew in feeling unappreciated and overworked or we can choose to take a different perspective.

I needed to be reminded of this today. I need a change in perspective. I'm so glad the Lord gives us all we need to fulfill what He has called us to do. This includes serving our homes and families. Will you join me in a perspective change today? Will you join me in seeing and doing all those tasks as unto the Lord? It won't be in vain, but it will please the Lord and lessen the burden.

Daily Declarations

I declare that I will serve my home and family as unto the Lord. I declare that I am making a shift in my perspective. I choose to serve with gladness.

Prayer Starter

Thank You Lord for the reminder. Thank You for helping me change my perspective. Thank You for knowing that the struggle is real, and for encouraging me in the middle of it. Help me to choose the right attitude and perspective every day. In Jesus' name, Amen.

journal

journal

Day 17

"He Stands Still"

Luke 18:35-43

"Then it happened, as He was coming near Jericho, that a certain blind man sat by the road begging. And hearing a multitude passing by, he asked what it meant. So they told him that Jesus of Nazareth was passing by. And he cried out, saying, 'Jesus, Son of David, have mercy on me!' Then those who went before warned him that he should be quiet; but he cried out all the more, 'Son of David, have mercy on me!' So Jesus stood still and commanded him to be brought to Him. And when he had come near, He asked him, saying, 'What do you want Me to do for you?' He said, 'Lord, that I may receive my sight.' Then Jesus said to him, 'Receive your sight; your faith has made you well.' And immediately he received his sight, and followed Him, glorifying God. And all the people, when they saw it, gave praise to God."

This is one of my favorite stories. Here is this blind man sitting on the side of the road begging. When he hears Jesus is near the desperation for a touch compels him to cry out for mercy. People tried to silence him yet their warning caused him to cry out even more. Desperation can be uncomfortable. People don't know how to handle it or what to do. In this case the people tried to silence it. Don't allow desperation to be silenced in you. Let your desperation for God and His presence be heard. Jesus hears it. Above the noise of the multitude Jesus hears the desperation of the cry of one man. My favorite part is just three words. Jesus stood still. I love this! With a multitude surrounding Him one man's cry caused Jesus to stand still. He still stands still. He stands still at the sound of your cry. He stands still at the sound of your worship. He sees the crowd, but He stands still for the individual. He is an individual God. He chooses to stand still, hear the desperation, and look upon the need of one. Not only did He stand still but He met him at the point of His need. He brought healing and the man received his sight. Desperation led to deliverance.

What are you desperate for today? What is it you need Jesus to stand still for? Jesus is near to where you are...right now. He is there. He sees you. He knows you. He is standing still. Tell Him what you need. Let your desperation lead to your deliverance.

Daily Declarations

Today's declarations are your choice. Declare your desperation. Declare what you need. Declare your deliverance.

Prayer Starter

Lord Jesus, Thank You for standing still at the sound of my cry. Thank You for seeing me, knowing me, and loving me. I am desperate for You.

journal

journal

Day 18
"Come Boldly"

Hebrews 4:15-16

"For we do not have a High Priest who cannot sympathize with our weaknesses, but was in all points tempted as we are, yet without sin. Let us therefore come boldly to the throne of grace, that we may obtain mercy and find grace to help in time of need."

What an amazing thing to know that our God, our Savior, our King experienced what we do. He knows what we feel and go through because He felt and experienced it too. He overcame the experiences without sin. He overcame it all so that we could walk in victory. When we are facing something, we don't have to come crawling and begging. We can walk right in with boldness because we know Jesus conquered all. Mercy and grace are waiting. An easy explanation of mercy and grace is: Mercy is not getting what you deserve and grace is getting what you don't deserve. Jesus conquered sin and death so that we could have both. Mercy and grace go hand in hand and they are waiting to help you in your time of need. All you have to do is come before the throne and receive. The battle has already been won. Jesus, our High Priest, is waiting to give you what you need.

What is it that you need? Come boldly! Mercy, grace, and Jesus are waiting. He knows what you have need of already. Come and ask. He longs to shower you with grace and mercy. He will give you the help you need. He is good and He has conquered all!

Daily Declarations

I declare that Jesus is the Mighty One. I declare that Jesus is my High Priest. I declare that I will come boldly before the throne of grace. I declare that I will find help in my time of need.

Prayer Starter

Lord, I come boldly to Your throne to receive grace and mercy. I honor You and praise You for who You are.

journal

journal

Day 19

"That Good Part"

Luke 10:38-42

"Now it happened as they went that He entered a certain village; and a certain woman named Martha welcomed Him into her house. And she had a sister called Mary, who also sat at Jesus' feet and heard His word. But Martha was distracted with much serving, and she approached Him and said, 'Lord, do You not care that my sister has left me to serve alone? Therefore tell her to help me. And Jesus answered and said to her, 'Martha, Martha, you are worried and troubled about many things. But one thing is needed and Mary has chosen that good part, which will not be taken away from her."

Do you recognize yourself in either Mary or Martha? I think if we are really being honest, we can say that we have been both Mary and Martha at different times in our lives. Mary is sitting at Jesus' feet and Martha is distracted. Here Martha has invited Jesus in and instead of recognizing the moment and resting in His presence, she is busy and distracted. She was busy with something good. She was serving Jesus. She was caught up in the doing and she allowed the doing to distract her from the sitting. Have you ever been invited to someone's house and they are so focused on serving you that they aren't with you? It's kind of awkward isn't it? Here you think you are going to spend time and build relationship and your host is too busy to sit with you. They are busy with good but they and you miss the good relationship part. This is what was happening. Martha got so caught up in the serving that she missed the good part. Her distraction then turned to accusation. She put her sister on blast and asked Jesus to reprimand her. Now this party just got even more awkward, but Jesus is so kind. It is an amazing thing when Jesus says your name. Martha was so riled up that Jesus says her name twice. He sees that she is stressed and worried. She's blaming her sister for not helping, yet Jesus calms her by saying her name and recognizing her struggle. He then reminds her of the main thing. Keep the main thing the main thing as the saying goes. Jesus is the main thing. Sitting at His feet and being in His presence. It's all about Him. Everything we do is for Him, but if we get caught up in the doing, that good thing is missed and the main thing is no longer the main thing. The doing has become the main thing. Without the presence of Jesus the doing has no meaning. When we keep Jesus the main thing, we can be at His feet, in His presence everywhere we go and in everything we do. The doing is then marked by the sitting. Our lives need to be marked by the sitting. Our lives need to reflect the times of sitting at Jesus feet in worship and marked by our relationship with Him. We can't miss "that good part". Our doing will just be doing without it. Worship determines the direction of your life. Stay at His feet wherever you are and in whatever you're doing. Don't become distracted. Let all you do be an expression of worship. Worship is a lifestyle, and it is living at His feet.

Daily Declarations

I declare that Jesus is the main thing. I declare that I will keep Jesus the main thing. I declare that I will live a life marked by sitting at the feet of Jesus. I declare that His presence is with me in all that I do. I declare that my doing is not a reflection of me but it is a reflection of Him.

Prayer Starter

Thank You Jesus for saying my name and reminding me that You are the main thing. I will stay at Your feet and in Your presence. I want my life to reflect that good part. I don't want to miss it. Help me to not be so caught in doing that I miss the sitting. Amen.

journal

journal

journal

Day 20
"Speak Truth"

Job 42:7-8

"And so it was, after the Lord had spoken these words to Job, that the Lord said to Eliphaz the Temanite, 'My wrath is aroused against you and your two friends, for you have not spoken of me what is right, as My servant Job has. Now therefore, take for yourselves seven bulls and seven rams, go to My servant Job, and offer up for yourselves a burnt offering; and My servant Job shall pray for you. For I will accept him, lest I deal with you according to your folly; because you have not spoken of Me what is right, as My servant Job has.'"

Let's be real, the book of Job isn't my go to book for encouragement or when I need a word from God. It is full of testing, suffering, grief, and woe. I was reading the book of Job as part of a daily reading plan that I was following. I usually try to get through it as fast as I can, but there is meat to be had in there. This particular piece of meat comes in the last chapter. I got to verses seven and eight and the Lord spoke so clear to me. He said, "It matters to me how you talk about Me". He cares how we speak about Him. It matters to Him that we speak the truth of who He is. Job's friends were not speaking rightly about God and it caused His wrath to be stirred towards them. They had to atone for the words they spoke about Him. They had to prepare a burnt offering and offer it before Job who had spoken rightly. Job was accepted because He spoke the truth about God.

Speaking the truth of who God is helps to build our faith. Knowing who He is and speaking the truth of who He is spurs us to believe that He is true to who He says He is and will do what He says He will do. It matters to Him because He wants us to believe Him and trust Him. How have you been speaking about Him? Have you been speaking what is right and true? Have your words been matching up to your belief or has your belief shrunk down to your words? It matters to Him how you speak about Him because how you speak about Him alters how you believe Him. Speak what is right of Him and your belief will follow.

Daily Declarations

I declare that I will speak the truth of who God is. I will speak what is right of Him. I declare that He is who He says He is. He is good. He is faithful.

Prayer Starter

Lord, forgive me for any time that I have not spoken of You what is right. Help my words to match my belief and for my belief to match my words if need be. In Jesus' name, Amen

journal

journal

Day 21
"In or Out?"

Matthew 14:22-33

v.28-31 "And Peter answered Him and said, 'Lord, if it is You, command me to come to You on the water.' So He said, 'Come'. And when Peter had come down out of the boat, he walked on the water to go to Jesus. But when he saw that the wind was boisterous, he was afraid; and beginning to sink he cried out, saying, 'Lord, save me!' and immediately Jesus stretched out His hand and caught him, and said to him, 'O you of little faith, why did you doubt?'"

I would have enjoyed knowing Peter. He is gutsy and bold. He was the only one of the disciples who had faith enough to get out of the boat. I like to imagine the things that aren't written in the stories of the Bible. I like to think about the human element and what the people involved were thinking and feeling. I wonder about Peter and the other disciples. Here they are in a boat out in the sea and here comes Jesus walking on the water. That had to have been a bit unnerving. They knew His voice so they knew it was Jesus. Peter dares to step out of the boat. All that was needed was the word "Come". Jesus says "come" and Peter steps down off the boat onto the water. I wonder how long it took him. Did he jump off the side or hesitantly climb over? What were the other disciples doing and saying? Were they trying to talk him out of it or were they curious to see if he could do it? It doesn't say, but I wonder about it. I think when he heard the word from Jesus he acted. I think he jumped over the side and started walking. I wonder how long he was walking before he started checking out the waves. How many steps had he taken? How far had he gotten? It doesn't say he immediately started to sink. It says "when he saw the wind was boisterous, he was afraid". He only started sinking when his focus switched from going towards Jesus to the storm that was surrounding him. It wasn't just that he saw the storm but he allowed fear to set in and the fear caused him to start sinking. Fear does that doesn't it? It grips you and it can feel as though you're unable to move forward. The beautiful thing is that as soon as he cried out to Jesus He was there. We don't know how far apart from each other they were. What we do know is that as soon as Peter cried, Jesus was there. He stretched out His hand and Peter was caught. Peter was already out of the boat. He had already been doing what no one but Jesus had ever done. He was walking on water. A moment of faith brought about the impossible; a moment of fear and doubt brought about a rescue.

Peter's lack of faith is typically the part of this story that is focused on. That how could he have taken his eyes off Jesus when he was already out there. I would like to focus on the incredible fact that he got out of the boat in the first place. He heard Jesus say "come" and he responded. He took the risk. He trusted Jesus to get out of the boat. He got out of the boat and did the impossible. We all have an on the water moment waiting for us. What is yours? What is God calling you to do that is going to take you trusting Him enough to get out of the boat? It is worth it. Take the risk, get out of the boat, and do the impossible.

Write down the things that God is calling You to do. Keep it before you and call those things that aren't as though they are.

91

Daily Declarations

I declare that I am a water walker! I declare
that I will get out of the boat, take the risk,
and do what God is calling me to do. I declare
that I am bold and courageous!

Prayer Starter

Jesus, I trust You. Thank You for calling me out
on the water. I choose to come when You call
and to trust You to walk with me.

journal

journal

journal

Day 22

"One Word"

Galatians 5:14

"For all the law is fulfilled in one word, even this: 'You shall love your neighbor as yourself'".

It is a powerful thing to think that everything we tend to strive for is fulfilled in one word. Simple but difficult at the same time. Love. Love is powerful and freeing. It takes the burden of striving off and makes things simple. Everything we try to fulfill in the law is settled with one word. Love. Walking in love is a choice. It is easier to walk with our own intentions and purposes in mind. Walking in love requires stepping outside of ourselves and caring about the needs of others. It's about walking the way Jesus would. The next verses deal with not walking according to the flesh. The word says the works of the flesh are evident. As I was reading this chapter I was struck by the thought that all sin, all works of the flesh are results of selfishness. All of the things listed are results of self. When we put on love and walk in it we put down selfishness and put on the Spirit. The fruits of the Spirit are results of walking in love. It all works together. The greatest definition of love is found in 1 Corinthians 13. We know it as the love chapter because the main focus is defining what love is. Love is patient, kind, not envious or selfish, not conceited, it rejoices in truth, it hopes and endures, it's not rude, it thinks good and not evil, it believes and it never ever fails. Sounds a lot like the fruit of the Spirit.

Walking in the Spirit and love is not always easy. There are days that are harder than others. It's those moments that are difficult when we really have to stop and choose love. The moments when we've been hurt, disappointed, frustrated, or displaced. Those moments give us the opportunity to choose love. To choose to see outside of ourselves and to put on the fruit of the Spirit. To choose to walk like Jesus. Jesus was all those things. Hurt, disappointed, frustrated, displaced, wrongly accused; yet in all of it He was the purest example of love. He faced all that we do and He can sympathize with us and knows what we are going through. It's not always easy, but it can be done. Each day we need to wake up and choose to walk in love. Some days it feels like it's moment to moment choices. Can I get an Amen?! Many days it's like this. The reality is that we choose how we respond to things. We choose to remain hurt, angry, and frustrated. All of these are very real feelings. I am not downplaying them for a moment. It's all in what we choose in those moments that determine our walk. I challenge you today to choose to walk in love in every situation you face. Choose love and the fruit of the Spirit. Ask the Lord for help in the moments that are difficult. He will give you the grace you need in the very moment you need it.

Daily Declarations

I declare that I am a person who walks in love. I declare that I am a person growing in the fruit of the Spirit. I declare that I will daily put on and choose love.

Prayer Starter

Lord, help me daily choose love. Help me to be like You in the situations I face today. Thank You for being the perfect example of love.

journal

journal

Day 23

"A Simple Thing"

Romans 8:31-32

"What then shall we say to these things? If God is for us, who can be against us? He who did not spare His own Son, but delivered Him up for us all, how shall He not with Him also freely give us all things?"

Anything we might face is a simple thing in light of the greatness of our God. I have been pondering this thought for a couple of days; "If God is for us, who can be against us?" Sometimes it feels like everything and everybody is coming against us all at once. The key I have discovered is in the question, "What shall we say to these things?" Too often when faced with circumstances, people problems, money problems, you name it-instead of asking these questions "What shall we say to these things?" and "Who can be against us?", we lay down under the weight of what we are facing. We lay down and accept the situation for what it is instead of proclaiming the truth-that God is for us so who can be against us?!

This doesn't mean that the situations and circumstances we face aren't real. They are. We face things every day; but when we are faced with these real things, what do we say to them? Do we speak the negativity of what's happening or do we speak the reality of what God says about what's happening? This is such a key thing to victory. Yes, you have to be real and honest and acknowledge what's happening, but victory comes in the realization that God is for you and that giant you're facing is a simple thing to Him. He is not taken by surprise or shocked that it's happening. He has already prepared for you what you need to get through it. He did not withhold His only Son from you. He, with Jesus, will freely give you all things. Wisdom, grace, mercy, patience, defense, justice, provision, healing. All of it is already prepared and waiting for you to grab hold of at the exact moment you need it. He is a good God. He is a good father. What will you say to the things you're facing? I challenge you to declare those things that aren't as though they are. Declare your victory. Write it out if you have to and put it in a prominent place. Keep it before your eyes and speak it out. Speak the truth over your situation. What shall you say to these things? God is for me, so who or what can be against me?!

Daily Declarations

I declare that God is for me! I declare that the thing I'm facing is a simple thing. I declare victory in every situation and circumstance I'm facing.

Prayer Starter

Lord, You are a good God and a good father. Thank You that the things I'm facing are not a surprise to You. Thank You for preparing all I need before I need it. I trust You and know that You hold me in Your hand. It is well with me.

journal

journal

Day 24

"Good Father"

Zephaniah 3:17

"The Lord your God in your midst; The Mighty One, will save; He will rejoice over you with gladness, He will quiet you with His love, He will rejoice over you with singing."

What a beautiful picture of the Father's love for us. There is so much in this verse that speaks to the deep places of our hearts. First He reminds us that He is with us, right in our midst. There are days when we don't necessarily "feel" Him and the enemy would want us to think He has forsaken us or that He's angry with us. How about this one-He's disappointed in us. Over and over in the Word the Lord reminds us that He will never leave us or forsake us, and here is another reminder. He is in our midst.

"The Mighty One will save." He is in our midst with all of His might ready to save. He gives us this reminder that He is the Mighty One. There is nothing so big or so bad that the Mighty One can't save you from. It doesn't say The Mighty One might save-No! It says the Mighty One will save! He can and will save you!

I love the next part of this verse. I think many times we have the mindset that yes He will save me, but He's going to be mad, upset, or dis- appointed with me. He so sweetly cancels that thought and fear with, "He will rejoice over you with gladness." After He saves us, He rejoices over us. While He rejoices over us, He then quiets us with His love. As I read this I got a picture of the Father holding a child and sweetly quiet- ing their cries and their fears. I thought of my little one when she is upset. As I hold her and quiet her she has a peace come over her because she is in my arms. It's the same for us with the Father. He holds us and He calms and quiets us with His love and peace. We have an amazing Father. He saves, rejoices, quiets, and sings. Yes, He sings over you. The Mighty One, the King of Kings, the Lord of lords-sings; and He sings over you. You are deeply loved. Your heavenly Father deeply loves you. He is with you, He rejoices over you with gladness and singing, and He quiets your anxieties and fears with His love. What a beautiful reminder. Rest in His love today, and rest in knowing that you have a good, good Father.

Daily Declarations

I declare that I am loved. I declare that my heavenly Father is a good father. I declare that His peace and love will hold me today. I choose to rest in Him knowing that He is good!

Prayer Starter

Thank You Father for Your great love for me. Thank You that no matter what I do or what I feel you are there loving me and ready to save. Help me to not doubt Your love for me, and help me to rest fully in You...

journal

journal

Day 25
"You Are A Good Work"

Philippians 1:6

"being confident of this very thing, that He who has begun a good work in you will complete it until the day of Jesus Christ"

Lately the Lord has had me in the letters from Paul: Galatians, Ephesians, and Philippians. These books are full, rich, and compelling. The truth of God's word compels us to maturity. These letters abound with choices that lead to our maturity in Christ. The choices lie in what we do with the word when we read it. How do we respond? Do we read it with the idea that we can be free and changed or do we read it thinking that we will never attain the kind of life Paul writes about? Do we believe what Philippians 1:6 says, "that He who has begun a good work in you will complete it until the day of Jesus Christ"? Do you believe that? Do you believe that God will complete the work in you? God never does anything half-way. From creation to redemption He completed and finished everything. Why would He not complete and finish the good work in you? He wouldn't! He is faithful and He will complete the work. The Scripture says, "He who began a <u>good</u> work..." This reminds me of creation. After everything He created God saw that it was good. He is in the business of creating good things and He is in the business of completing those good things. He only rested when He was finished. Jesus cried out "It is finished" right before He gave up His spirit. From creation to redemption it's finished. The work He is working in us is a good work and it will be completed. We can trust in His ability and desire to continue to work in us until we see Him face to face. Aren't you glad?! Aren't you glad He didn't leave you to figure it out on your own?! He will complete you! He will fulfill the good work in you!

Choose to trust Him to continue the work in you. Don't give up! You are a good thing that He is molding and fashioning. An artist looks over their work and continues to add, take away, and edit until the masterpiece is before them. You are His masterpiece. Allow Him to continue working in you until you are complete.

Daily Declarations

I declare that I am His masterpiece. I declare that God will complete the good work He has begun in me. I declare that God does all things well and that includes me!

Prayer Starter

Thank You Lord for Your ability to finish the good work. Thank You that You have chosen me and that You are fashioning me into the masterpiece You have dreamed in Your heart. I trust You to complete me and I trust You in the process. In Jesus' name, Amen.

journal

journal

Day 26

"A Forever Love"

Romans 9:38-39

"For I am persuaded that neither death nor life, nor angels nor principalities, nor powers, nor things present, nor things to come, nor height nor depth, nor any other created thing, shall be able to separate us from the love of God which is in Christ Jesus our Lord."

The love of God is as infinite as He is. It is forever. Nothing and nobody can separate His love from us. Nothing we do, no shame, no wrong choice-nothing will keep us from His love. His love for you caused Him to send His son to die for you. Do you think there is anything you could possibly do that would cause him to remove that love from you? He loves you beyond life and death. Nothing you have ever done or will ever do can keep you from His love. No circumstance and certainly no power from hell will keep you from His love. The enemy would want to get you thinking that the Father's love for you is somehow dependent on you. Your actions, motives, or beliefs have nothing to do with whether He loves you or not. This type of thinking belittles the love of God and really God Himself. The Word says that He IS love. So to question His love for you is to really question who He is.

How do we combat against this thinking?

By having a revelation of who He is and of His love. He promised to never leave us or forsake us. So, knowing He is, in His very nature, love-doesn't it stand to reason that His love will never leave us or forsake us as well? His love for You caused Him to pay the ultimate price. Having paid that price, He will not draw back or remove the very love that cost Him so much.

He loves you. He loves you with all that He is. He loved you while still in your sin. He loved you before you breathed your first breath. He stays the same…yesterday, today, and forever; and because He doesn't change, His love doesn't change.

I pray that you will have a revelation of his love for you. Take some time and write down the areas of your life where you need a revelation of His love. Trust Him and trust His love for you.

Daily Declarations

I declare that God is the same yesterday, today, and forever. I declare that He is love and because He doesn't change, His love doesn't change. I declare that I AM LOVED! I renounce the lie that He loves me with conditions. I renounce the lie that I have to earn His love. I choose today to trust His love for me.

Prayer Starter

Thank You Lord for loving me. Thank You that Your love never fails and that Your love will never be taken away from me. I ask for a revelation of Your love in every area of my life. Thank You that I am able to love because You love me.

journal

journal

Day 27

"Time to Dream"

2 Corinthians 8:10-11

"And in this I give advice: It is to your advantage not only to be doing what you began and were desiring to do a year ago; but now you also must complete the doing of it; that as there was a readiness to desire it, so there also may be a completion out of what you have."

The Word really is an instruction manual for our lives. It acts as a mirror, a dictionary to define who we are, and a day in and day out guide for life. What are the dreams of your heart? What are the things you wanted to do? What are the things you started and didn't finish? What are those things that you laid down because circumstances changed or your role in life changed?

I believe we are in a season of dreams being brought back to life. Those things you dared to dream but never saw come to fruition...the time has come to dream again. God gives us desires and dreams not so that we live disappointed or always feeling like we never quite hit the mark, but those desires are to be fulfilled. He doesn't only give you the desire but He gives you everything you need to complete and fulfill it. What is stopping you from completing those things? What is it you need to reach your goal? I heard it said once, "If it's God's will, it's God's bill!" This doesn't only mean money. Whatever is needed He will provide. Strength, energy, finances, connections, ideas, revelation. Whatever is needed.

Take some time and write down the things you once desired yet never finished. Write down the dreams and desires of your heart. Present them to the Lord. He will help you finish and finish well. Dare to dream again. Regardless of the circumstances of life, dare to dream.

Regardless of your abilities or lack there-of...dare to dream. Ask the Lord to revive the dream He placed in your heart. He will complete every good work in you including the dreams He has put in you.

Daily Declarations

I declare that I am a dreamer. I declare that I will finish well. I declare that the things that have laid dormant will spring back to life. I declare that the things I have desired and started will be completed.

Prayer Starter

Lord, I commit the desires and dreams of my heart to You. Help me to dream again. Help me to not hold back because of the circumstances of my life. I commit to finishing the things You have called me to...

journal

journal

Day 28
"Identity in Covenant"

1 Samuel 17:26

"Then David spoke to the men who stood by him, saying, 'What shall be done for the man who kills this Philistine and takes away the reproach from Israel? For who is this uncircumcised Philistine, that he should defy the armies of the living God?'"

The story of David and Goliath is one of my favorites, and this verse is my favorite part of the story. Yes, I love the action of the fight. I can almost see it as a movie playing in my mind as I read it. David stoops down to choose the stones as the music plays. He places a stone in his sling, and he slowly starts winding up. As the music builds he winds faster and faster until the music hits the ultimate crescendo. The music falls silent as he releases the stone. It soars through the air and rests, implanted in the forehead of Goliath. Goliath slowly falls straight back and lands with a thud and dust rising from the ground. It an extremely dramatic and exciting scene. The fight and victory is amazing, but it's not my favorite part. My favorite part is when David says, "who is this uncircumcised Philistine..." You may wonder why this is my favorite part. It is my favorite because this statement speaks of identity. David knew the difference between his and Goliath's identities. The difference had nothing to do with stature, nationality, or age. It had everything to do with covenant. David recognized that his identity was forged in covenant with the Living God. He declared the truth of the situation. "Who is this uncircumcised Philistine?" David is saying, who is this that has no covenant? Who does he think he is defying the armies of the Lord?

Here we have David, a youth, being fully aware of who he is, who he's in covenant with, and what that covenant means. David won the battle because he knew and was confident in his identity. He fully trusted God to make good on His covenant. We are in covenant with the same God as David. In fact, the Word says that we have a better covenant. Knowing your identity will lead to your victory.

What is the giant you are facing? What is that thing that would dare to defy the child of the living God? You can look that thing in the face and declare the truth. Your stones are the promises of God. The truth of who you are and the truth of who your covenant partner is. The word says that "all of the promises of God, in Him, are yes and in Him Amen!" That means that all of them are already done because of Jesus. You are in covenant with the Almighty, Living God, and with that covenant comes everything you need for life, godliness, and giant slaying. Know who you are. Speak the truth of your identity. Dig in the Scriptures and allow the Holy Spirit to show you who you are. Your identity will lead to your victory!

Daily Declarations

I declare that I am in covenant with the Almighty God. I declare that I am a child of God and that all of His promises for me are yes and Amen. I declare that He is for me. I declare that I know who I am and whose I am.

Prayer Starter

Thank You Lord for Your covenant. Thank You that victory is in my identity. Help me to never doubt, question, or forget who I am in You.

journal

journal

Day 29
"Peace Be Still"

Philippians 4:8

"Finally, brethren, whatever things are true, whatever things are noble, whatever things are just, whatever things are pure, whatever things are lovely, whatever things are of good report, if there is any virtue and if there is anything praiseworthy-meditate on these things."

There are times when things come our way that seem to overtake our minds. Work pressures, illness, finances, relationship struggles, school pressure, deadlines, kids, and the list could go on and on. We live in a world where things are changing fast and times seem to move faster than we can keep up. God is so good that He gave us this verse to bring clarity to all that would want to flood and occupy our minds. We can break away from the stress and pressure and fill our minds with all that God is. He is true. He is noble. He is good. He is pure. He is lovely. He brings a good report. He is virtuous, and He is definitely worthy of praise.

Hardships are guaranteed to come. Pressure, worry, fear, stress, illness. We all face these things but we don't have to be overcome by them. We can acknowledge that they're happening, but keep our thoughts and hearts turned toward the Lord. He makes all things beautiful. He turns mourning into dancing. He supplies all of our needs. He keeps us in perfect peace. His perfect love casts out fear. He gives wisdom generously. We are healed by His stripes.

I don't know what you are facing. I do know that God is good. We have had quite a few days where He has spoken to us regarding situations and giants we are facing. I know I am facing some. He is so good to keep reminding us of His great love for us and His desire that we would be guarded by His peace.

My amazing friend Anna wrote a beautiful song called Peace Be Still. This song has become a rock for me as I have listened to it and sang it in some of the most difficult times of my life. Some of the words are: "And You keep saying, 'Peace, be still, know that I am God who will; carry you from day to day'...'I'll trust in You and I will obey'. I believe the Lord is saying this to us today. Peace be still. He is God and He will carry us day to day. Our only response then is to trust him and obey.

Daily Declarations

I declare that my mind is stayed on good things. I declare that God is good and that He keeps me in perfect peace. I declare that I will trust and obey.

Prayer Starter

Lord, Thank You for Your great love for me and for Your perfect peace. Thank You that I can draw near to You when times are hard and when times are good. I choose to keep my mind meditating on all that You are.

journal

journal

Day 30
"Hear and Receive"

Ezekiel 3:10

"Moreover He said to me: 'Son of man, receive into your heart all My words that I speak to you, and hear with your ears.'"

It is so evident throughout the Word that hearing and receiving go hand in hand. It is easy to hear the Word of the Lord; whether His written Word, or His spoken Word to us individually, and to believe it is for someone else. It is easy to hear the word and not receive it for ourselves, our lives, and situations. God is calling us to not only hear the Word with our ears but to receive it into our hearts. The receiving activates the hearing. When we receive His Word into our hearts it can take root and grow. His Word is not idle talk or a work of fiction, but it is life. It is active. It is current and it is life changing. It needs to take root and grow.

What are the words He has spoken to you lately? What have you heard and read that you need to receive and activate? Activate the Word by receiving it in your heart as a gift to you. When someone gives you a gift, you don't leave it in their hands and stare at it. No, you receive it, open it and take ownership of it. The same is true with the words and promises of God. We aren't to just look at them and admire them. We are to receive them, open them, and take ownership of them. They belong to you. His Words are gifts; hear them and receive them. Activate your hearing by receiving.

Take some time and write down the Words you need activated. Be intentional and receive what you are hearing.

I pray that these last 29 days have brought you closer to the God who loves you so much. I hope you have enjoyed your coffee with Jesus as much as I have. Keep it up. He has much more for you than you can think or imagine.

Daily Declarations

I declare God's Word is a gift. I declare that I receive His Word and I declare that my hearing and faith are activated. I declare that His Word will come to pass in my life.

Prayer Starter

Lord, Thank You for the gift of Your Word. I receive what You are saying to me. Help me to not only receive but believe it.

journal

journal

Made in the USA
San Bernardino, CA
19 July 2017